QUARTERBACK POWER

by Tim Polzer

Dear Carson,
  Happy 5½ Birthday!
Enjoy the book and
your special day! :)
            Mr. Pechous

SCHOLASTIC INC.

New York   Toronto   London   Auckland   Sydney
Mexico City   New Delhi   Hong Kong   Buenos Aires

ISBN 0-439-69179-6

Published by Scholastic Inc.
SCHOLASTIC and associated logos are trademarks
and/or registered trademarks of Scholastic Inc.

12 11 10 9 8 7 6 5 4 3   4 5 6 7 8/0

Designed by Rick DeMonico

Printed in the U.S.A.
First printing, September 2004

Chapter One

TOM BRADY

Tom Brady is one of the most accurate and consistent quarterbacks in the National Football League, but he took an unusual path to stardom. Just when it seemed that Tom would spend his career sitting on the New England Patriots' bench, he got into a game and showed people how well he could play. Tom surprised everyone by becoming one of the league's best quarterbacks and winning two Super Bowls in three seasons.

Tom grew up in San Mateo, California, where he enjoyed playing sports. He was a good athlete who played football and baseball at the same high school as Pro Football Hall of Fame receiver Lynn Swann, and Major League Baseball home run king Barry Bonds. Tom played catcher on his high school baseball team and was good enough to be drafted by the Montreal Expos in 1995.

Instead of playing professional baseball, Tom chose to play football in college. He accepted a football scholarship to the University of Michigan, where the Wolverines won 20 of 25 games with Tom as their starting quarterback. He was also a backup quarterback to Brian Griese on the Wolverines' 1997 national championship team.

Though Tom played well in college, he was not expected to be a great NFL quarterback. He was not selected until the sixth round of the 2000 NFL Draft. Many players were chosen before him, but he did not give up.

Tom had to sit on the bench as the Patriots' third-string quarterback, but his coaches noticed how hard he worked to learn the team's offense. Head coach Bill Belichick soon made Tom the team's second-string quarterback, but Tom was not satisfied. He kept practicing and working until he improved even more.

When Drew Bledsoe, the Patriots' starting quarterback, was injured early in the 2001 season, Tom was finally given a chance to play. He played very well, leading the Patriots to 14 wins in 17 games. He also set an NFL record for most pass attempts (162) to start a career without throwing an interception.

Tom became very good at reading the other team's defense, finding an open receiver, and throwing the ball to the right spot. He helped his team by not making many mistakes. When the game was on the line, Tom usually played very well and he did not get upset under pressure.

Tom's consistent play helped the Patriots win the American Football Conference East Division in 2001. In the play-offs, Tom helped the Patriots beat the Oakland Raiders in overtime in a blizzard. He got hurt in the AFC Championship Game against Pittsburgh, but Coach Belichick thought he had earned the right to be the Patriots' starting quarterback in Super Bowl XXXVI.

In his first Super Bowl, Tom's reputation for playing extremely well under pressure was born. With one minute and twenty-one seconds left in the game, the Patriots were tied 17–17 with the favored St. Louis Rams. Tom led his team down the field to set up the game-winning field goal by kicker Adam Vinatieri.

For his heroics, Tom was awarded the Pete Rozelle Trophy as the Most Valuable Player of Super Bowl XXXVI. At 24 years and 184 days old, Tom was the youngest quarterback to win a Super Bowl, more than a year younger than the New York Jets' Joe Namath and the San Francisco 49ers' Joe Montana.

Two years later, Tom and the Patriots finished with the best record in the NFL. In Super Bowl XXXVIII, Tom played well again, completing a Super Bowl-record 32 passes against the Carolina Panthers, one more than Pro Football Hall of Fame member Jim Kelly.

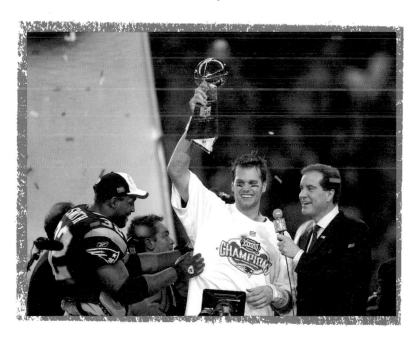

Tom again led the Patriots to a last-minute victory, driving the team for another game-winning field goal in the final seconds. It was the fourteenth time in just three seasons that Tom had led the Patriots to a come-from-behind victory. For his efforts, Tom again was named the Super Bowl Most Valuable Player and awarded his second Pete Rozelle Trophy.

Many people compare Tom to Joe Montana, one of the NFL's greatest quarterbacks ever. Like Tom, Joe was not expected to be a great NFL quarterback, but he won four Super Bowls and directed many come-from-behind wins before retiring and entering the Pro Football Hall of Fame. Tom appreciates the compliment but knows that he must keep working hard to get the Patriots back to the Super Bowl.

Chapter Two

BRETT FAVRE

Brett Favre is a southerner who did not become one of the greatest NFL quarterbacks of all time until he moved north to Green Bay, Wisconsin. Green Bay is home to the famous Packers football team that won many NFL championships in the league's earlier days. Green Bay is smaller than most NFL cities, but its fans are known for be-

ing very passionate and supportive. The Packers owned a great history, but the team had suffered through a long slump until Brett became their quarterback.

Brett grew up in tiny Kiln, Mississippi. As a boy, he learned to hunt and fish the area's woods and swamps. Brett's father, Irv, was a high school football coach who taught his sons how to play. Brett became a football and baseball star at his high school and accepted a football scholarship to the University of Southern Mississippi.

Brett set many passing records at Southern Miss and caught the attention of NFL scouts. The Atlanta Falcons thought Brett would be a good quarterback so they picked him in the second round of the 1991 NFL Draft. Brett only took a few snaps in his rookie season. His Atlanta head coach did not think Brett was working or studying hard enough to be a starting quarterback so the team traded him to Green Bay in 1992. Having learned his lesson, Brett decided to take advantage of this new opportunity and dedicate himself to becoming the Packers' starting quarterback. He got that job in

his first season as a Packer, starting 13 games and passing for more than 3,000 yards and 18 touchdowns. He was even voted to the Pro Bowl in his first year as a starting quarterback.

Brett's breakthrough season turned out to be only the first of many record-setting performances that always included a dose of emotion and fun. Fans noticed that Brett, in kidlike fashion, always had fun when he played. Brett's enthusiasm and smile quickly made him a favorite in the north and across the country. He even enjoyed kidding with opposing defenders!

Brett has won an NFL-record three Most Valuable Player awards and is ranked among the top 10 in many NFL career

passing statistics. Brett also has thrilled fans with his habit of leading the Packers to dramatic come-from-behind wins. Through his thirteenth NFL season, Brett had led the Packers to 28 comeback victories after they were behind or tied in the fourth quarter.

Brett may be most famous for leading Green Bay back to the Super Bowl. In 1996, Brett and the Packers played in Super Bowl XXXI, where they defeated the New England Patriots. It was the Packers' first NFL championship in 29 years. Brett also quarterbacked the Packers to five division titles and nine playoff berths, including a second Super Bowl appearance. He has been voted to the Pro Bowl eight times.

Fans have enjoyed watching Brett's confident swagger week after week. In fact, fans have seen him play every week because he has never missed a game due to an injury. Favre's record-setting streak of starts was tested late in the 2003 season when his father died unexpectedly. Even though Brett was very sad and missed his father badly, he believed that Irv would have wanted him to play. Brett put his emotions aside and concentrated on the game at hand. As a national television audience watched, Brett played one of the best games of his career, passing for almost 400 yards and five touchdowns. In the game, Brett moved into second place for all-time touchdown passes and extended his NFL record to 205 consecutive starts by a quarterback. After the game, Brett dedicated the victory to his late father.

Even when Brett was at his lowest, his love for playing football was shared with his teammates and his many fans.

Chapter Three

PEYTON MANNING

Football has always been a family affair for Peyton Manning. Peyton's father, Archie, was a famous NFL quarterback for 15 years. He was also a very good quarterback at the University of Mississippi. As a professional, he was known for his passing and scrambling ability while playing for the New Orleans Saints, Houston Oilers, and Minnesota

Vikings. Archie was named the NFL's Most Valuable Player in 1978 and was voted to two Pro Bowls.

Peyton's younger brother, Eli, also played college football for Ole Miss and was the first player picked in the 2004 NFL Draft. He plays for the New York Giants. Peyton's older brother, Cooper, also played college football at Ole Miss before an injury forced him to stop.

Peyton played high school football in New Orleans. Since Archie had played at Ole Miss, many people wanted—and expected—Peyton to play college football in Mississippi. Peyton visited several colleges and thought carefully before deciding to play at the University of Tennessee.

Peyton was the Volunteers' starting quarterback during his four years at Tennessee. While there, he set a number of NCAA, conference, and school records. He also studied hard and earned Academic All-American honors.

The Indianapolis Colts selected Peyton with the first overall pick in the 1998 NFL Draft. He became the Colts' starting quarterback right away, passing for more then 3,700 yards

and 26 touchdowns in his rookie season. But he also threw 28 interceptions that season, so he worked hard on recognizing defensive coverages during the off-season.

Peyton's efforts paid off. He has been voted to the Pro Bowl four times and became the only NFL quarterback to total at least 3,000 passing yards in each of his first five seasons. He passed for more than 24,000 yards and 167 touchdowns in his first six NFL seasons.

Peyton's favorite target is Pro Bowl receiver Marvin Harrison. In their first six seasons together, Peyton has completed 527 passes to Marvin. The pair has combined for the most touchdown passes by an active duo.

His teammates and coaches recognize Peyton's dedication to the team and the game of football. He learned from his father and coaches that studying his team's offense as well as the tendencies of upcoming opposing defenses is the mark of a great quarterback and leader.

Despite Peyton's obvious statistical achievements, some NFL fans questioned his leadership. Going into the 2003 NFL season, Peyton had quarterbacked the Colts to many wins and three playoff berths, but he and his teammates had yet to win a playoff game. Football is a team game, but the quarterback often receives much of the criticism. Peyton heard the critics. He had heard the same questions when

Tennessee could not win a national championship with him as its quarterback. Could he perform in the clutch, when a playoff game was on the line?

Instead of getting upset, Peyton decided to work even harder. In 2003, Peyton helped lead the Colts to the playoffs for the fourth time and was named the NFL's co-MVP with Tennessee Titans quarterback Steve McNair. Peyton's new head coach, Tony Dungy, also was looking to end a playoff drought. He was 2–4 in previous playoff games while coaching Tampa Bay, and had lost three in a row.

Peyton and Tony ended their playoff streak, and the whispers, by defeating the Denver Broncos, 41–10. Peyton played one of the best games of his career, throwing touchdown passes on his team's first four possessions and giving the Colts an insurmountable lead. When the game ended,

he had connected on 22 of 26 passes for 377 yards and five touchdowns, and had earned a perfect passer rating of 158.3.

Peyton's family football roots helped teach him to overcome adversity and that hard work pays off. During the off-season, he tries to teach the same lessons to future quarterbacks at the Manning family summer football passing camp. He also has teamed with his father to write a book about their relationship and the family's football history. In that book, Archie Manning taught his sons one important lesson: Always finish what you start. Peyton hopes to finish an impressive NFL career with a Super Bowl victory.

DONOVAN MCNABB

Donovan McNabb had a rough start to his professional career, but since then he has run circles around NFL defenses and the many people who thought he couldn't be a great quarterback.

Philadelphia fans attending the 1999 NFL Draft in New York booed when the Eagles chose Donovan in the first

round. They wanted the team to choose a running back so they were not happy to hear Donovan's name called instead.

Donovan was disappointed by the greeting, but he did not let himself get down and he did not give up. He knew that he would change the minds of Philadelphia fans if given the chance. Donovan went to work, practiced hard, and became a good NFL quarterback. Now he does not hear any more boos. Philadelphia fans have changed their minds because Donovan has become one of the NFL's best and most exciting quarterbacks.

Donovan learned to work hard while growing up in Chicago, Illinois. He went to the same high school as NFL defensive end Simeon Rice, and Antoine Walker of the National Basketball Association. Donovan made many high school all-star teams, and he was offered a scholarship to play at Syracuse University in New York.

Donovan was good enough to start all four years at Syracuse. Not many college quarterbacks start all four years. He also played on the Orangemen's basketball team. Very few college athletes are good enough to play two sports.

Because Donovan's speed allowed him to run the ball just as well as he could throw it, he set many Syracuse and Big East Conference records for total offense, including a combined 9,950 yards of passing and rushing.

It was Donovan's leadership ability and his running and passing skills that led the Eagles to select him. His all-around talents allowed him to become the team's starter in his second season. Since then, Donovan has led the Eagles to four playoff berths and three straight appearances in the NFC Championship Game in four seasons as a starter.

As one of the NFL's most dangerous playmakers, Donovan scares defenses. When he drops back to pass, he is quick enough to scramble around the pass pocket, evading pass rushers while he waits for his receivers to get open. If no one is open, Donovan is fast enough to tuck the ball under his arm and race through the defense for a touchdown.

At 6-foot-2, 240 pounds, Donovan is larger and stronger than most NFL quarterbacks. His size is matched only by his toughness. In one game, Donovan led the Eagles to a win over the Arizona Cardinals while playing on an injured ankle. He would not let the injury stop him from helping his

team win that day, even though it forced him to miss the next six games.

Donovan also has a soft side. He has appeared along with his mom, Wilma, in popular Campbell's soup commercials on television. She is his number-one fan and has supported her son throughout his entire life. She also taught her son to help others. Donovan dresses up as Santa Claus and hands out gifts and toys to needy kids in Philadelphia every year. His charity, the Donovan McNabb Foundation, donates time and money to worthy causes every year, too.

Donovan is one of the Eagles' team leaders. He leads by example, working hard, studying his playbook, and watching videotape of upcoming opponents. While Donovan is serious about being the best football player he can be, he also has a good sense of humor. He likes to make his coaches and teammates laugh when they're not working hard. He hopes that he and the Eagles will soon be laughing after a Super Bowl victory.

CHAD PENNINGTON

Chad Pennington is not a flashy quarterback, but his ability to lead the New York Jets to victories reminds many fans of another larger-than-life NFL great.

In 1968, quarterback Joe Namath guaranteed that the Jets would be the first American Football League team to beat the older NFL's best team. When Joe made good on his promise, leading the Jets to a victory over the Baltimore Colts in Super Bowl III, a Pro Football Hall of Fame legend was born. Many Jets fans believe Chad is another quarterback legend in the making.

Chad cannot throw the football as far or as hard as Peyton Manning or Brett Favre. He cannot run as fast as Donovan McNabb or Michael Vick. Chad makes the best of his abilities by working hard and being smart. He almost always knows which Jets receiver will be open and when, and he is a very accurate passer.

Chad grew up in Knoxville, Tennessee, where he played football and basketball. After graduating from high school with excellent grades, he accepted a scholarship to play football at Marshall University in West Virginia, where Minnesota Vikings receiver Randy Moss was one of his teammates. At Marshall, Chad set team and conference records for touchdown passes and passing yards. Chad and Moss even set an NCAA record for most touchdown passes by a quarterback-receiver duo.

Based on his college performance, the Jets chose Chad in the first round of the 2000 NFL Draft. He was the Jets' third-string quarterback during his rookie season and mostly sat on the bench during his second season. Four games into his third season, Jets head coach Herm Edwards decided to let Chad start a game. He played well enough to become the starting quarterback for the rest of the season.

Chad threw to the right spots and made few mistakes in his first season as a starter. He set a new team record for completion percentage, completing more than 4 of every 5 passes. He also finished with the NFL's highest quarterback rating, a combination of passing statistics.

Chad's playmaking and leadership helped jump-start the Jets to the AFC East division title and a berth in the playoffs. On the way to the playoffs, Chad was a hero in a game against the New England Patriots that the Jets had to win. With the score tied 17–17 in the fourth quarter, he led the Jets on three straight scoring drives, passing for 285 yards and three touchdowns. In the minds of Jets fans, he had become almost as famous as Joe Namath.

Chad's excellent study habits are a big key to his success. He works hard learning the Jets' offense and watching videotape of opponents that can help him predict what they will do next. He learned that an education was important when he was just a kid.

Chad was a very good student in high school and college. He studied journalism at Marshall and finished with a 3.8 grade point average. Chad won many student-athlete awards and was a finalist for a Rhodes Scholarship to Oxford University in England.

Chad missed much of the 2003 season with a broken left wrist. Luckily, it was not his throwing wrist. He returned to play in the final ten games of the season.

With Chad back on the field, the Jets and their fans know that his intelligence and preparation, combined with his playmaking abilities, can lead them to the playoffs again and perhaps the team's first Super Bowl appearance since Joe Namath made his famous guarantee come true.

Chapter Six

MICHAEL VICK

Michael Vick is a multi-threat quarterback and one of the NFL's most exciting players. He has great strength and speed. After a trying rookie season, Michael has shown Atlanta Falcons fans that he is more than a great athlete. He is a great quarterback, too.

Michael grew up in Newport News, Virginia, which is also the hometown of NBA great Allen Iverson. Michael's cousin is New Orleans Saints quarterback Aaron Brooks. While growing up, Michael learned to do some unusual things, like throwing the football with his left hand, but doing every-thing else with his right hand.

Michael's athletic ability drew the attention of fans and NFL scouts when he played college football at Virginia Tech. His quickness and speed made him a dangerous runner and his strong arm allowed him to throw passes deep downfield. When Michael had the ball, defensive players didn't know what he would do next. He could scramble away from pass rushers and run away from tacklers.

Michael's abilities helped Virginia Tech win 20 games and lose only one in two seasons. Michael even led the Hokies to the National Championship Game but they lost to Florida State.

When Michael entered the 2001 NFL Draft, the Fal-cons thought his talent was great enough to take a big chance. Atlanta traded three draft choices and another player to the San Diego Chargers for the top pick. Football fans were very excited about his future. Michael's jersey was the sixth-best seller among all NFL player jerseys in his rookie season. He was the only rookie to have his jersey rank among the NFL's top 10 in sales.

   While everyone knew Michael was a potential superstar, no one knew for sure if he could become a great quarterback. Michael learned the Falcons' offensive system in practice and sat on the bench during games. When an injury to the Falcons' starting quarterback allowed Michael to play in eight games, he was inconsistent, sometimes playing well and other times playing poorly.

   Michael's rookie season was okay, but something happened during the offseason. He learned from his up-and-down experience, and when the season began he was ready to be a starting quarterback.

In just his second season, and first as a starter, Michael ignited the Falcons to a 9–6–1 record and their first playoff appearance in three seasons. Falcons fans reacted by buying all the tickets to every home game at the Georgia Dome for the first time in 10 years.

Michael not only showed fans that he could run the Falcons' offense, he also put up numbers that made him a Most Valuable Player candidate. He passed for almost 3,000 yards and ran for almost 1,000.

Michael led the Falcons to several come-from-behind wins, including an unforgettable performance against Minnesota. He single-handedly led the Falcons to an overtime win over the Vikings, rushing for 173 yards—a record for NFL quarterbacks—on just 10 carries. In overtime, Michael tucked the ball under his arm and sprinted back and forth across the field, eluding Vikings defenders on an amazing 46-yard game-winning touchdown run. It was one of the NFL's most exciting individual performances of all time.

Michael made more history when he led the Falcons over the Green Bay Packers in their Wild Card playoff game at Lambeau Field. It was the first time the Packers had ever lost a home playoff game.

Michael and the Falcons were disappointed when a leg injury forced him to miss much of the 2003 season, but everyone believes Michael has the potential to lead his team to a Super Bowl.

The Falcons' fans are ready. In Michael's second season, fans made his number 7 jersey the best-selling one among all NFL players.